So Hoo Hoo ~

COWLEY PUBLICATIONS is a ministry of the brothers of the Society of Saint John the Evangelist, a monastic order in the Episcopal Church. Our mission is to provide books and resources for those seeking spiritual and theological formation. COWLEY PUBLICATIONS is committed to developing a new generation of writers and teachers who will encourage people to think and pray in new ways about spirituality, reconciliation, and the future.

With love and full joy —
I hope this Book
Brings you great peace?

XXOOG
wilja

On Our Way Home

On Our Way Home

COURAGE AND FAITH FOR THE FINAL JOURNEY

Bob Herhold

Cowley Publications

CAMBRIDGE, MASSACHUSETTS

Published in the United States of America by Cowley Publications, a division of the Society of Saint John the Evangelist. No portion of this book may be reproduced, stored in or introduced into a retrieval system, or transmitted, in any form or by any means—including photocopying—without the prior written permission of Cowley Publications, except in the case of brief quotations embedded in critical articles and reviews.

Library of Congress Cataloging-in-Publication Data:

Herhold, Robert M.
  On our way home : courage and faith for the final journey / Bob Herhold.
     p. cm.
  Includes bibliographical references.
  ISBN-10: 1-56101-243-2 ISBN-13: 978-156101-243-5 (pbk. : alk. paper) 1. Older persons—Religious life. 2. Aging—Religious aspects—Christianity. 3. Death—Religious aspects—Christianity.
  I. Title.

BV4580.H37 2006
248.8′5—dc22

                                                        2005027103

Bible quotations are from the Revised Standard Version of the Bible, copyright 1952 [2nd edition, 1971] by the Division of Christian Education of the National Council of the Churches of Christ in the United States of America. Used by permission. All rights reserved.

Cover photo and design: Gary Ragaglia
Interior design: Wendy Holdman

This book was printed in the United States of America on acid-free paper.

Cowley Publications
4 Brattle Street
Cambridge, Massachusetts 02138
800-225-1534 • www.cowley.org

TO MURIEL,
GOD'S SMILE

CONTENTS

On Our Way Home

WHEN LIFE CRASHES

We must work the works of him
who sent me,
while it is day; night comes,
when no one can work.

JOHN 9:4

It came like a sudden unpredictable Midwest tornado. I sat at the edge of the bed, and as I started to stand up, I felt a sharp pain in my lower back. The pain subsided enough for my wife and me to fly to Denver for a family reunion. When we arrived, the pain returned and we flew home the next day.

X-rays and MRIs revealed compression fractures in the vertebrae of my lower back. This involved trips to several doctors and two brief stays in the hospital. My doctor prescribed a narcotic for pain—later the successful withdrawal from it was almost as troubling as the crushed vertebrae.

The recovery is much too slow for me; I am not naturally a patient man. I pound at the door of heaven and ask, "What's going on here? Where are you, God? Why are you so subtle, silent, and slow? How long will all this go on? Will I fall, or will another vertebra just snap like before?"

It is not a choice between medical science and prayer, anymore than it is between food and air. I find myself praying, "without ceasing," like "sighs too deep for words." Family and friends pray daily for me—a devout niece chants Buddhist prayers every morning for my health. With all of this, I still have problems; but without prayer, life would be emotionally and physically impossible.

God does not answer all my prayers. The truth is that my prayers are usually a laundry list of what needs God's attention. I often forget to thank God for the guidance and care in the past. Prayer is much more than mind can imagine or words describe.

I am like an old car—fix one thing and something else breaks down. Though I am in better shape than most people on the face of the earth, I still feel like I have donated my body to medical research. Here I am, a young guy wondering how he got trapped in an old geezer's body. As Charlie Brown would say, "The theological implications are staggering!"

Through many dangers, toils and snares,
I have already come;
'Tis grace has brought me safe thus far,
and grace will lead me home.

from "Amazing Grace"

By grace, the car keeps clunking along. I cannot believe that God, after seeing us through many struggling and joyful years, would simply total us.

WAYNE

It was September 12, 1975, and I had just settled in for a TV movie when the phone rang.
It was my younger brother, Wayne, who the
month before had accepted his dream job as
chief administrator of St. Luke's, a large hospital in downtown Denver. Like people who
want to climb Mt. Everest, Wayne jumped
at the challenge of bringing a dying hospital
back to life. More important than its finan-
cial crisis was the sinking morale of its staff.
Wayne charged in, eager for the challenge,
until he was stopped in his tracks.

After the usual banter about work and
families, Wayne said matter-of-factly that
he had been diagnosed with a blood disease,
similar to what took our dad. He talked about
it as if Geritol would fix everything up. We
both knew that Dad had a long hard battle,
with over two hundred blood transfusions.

I found myself that night on the 9:30 United flight to Denver. Once aboard, I felt a little foolish. I must be overreacting; maybe it's a mistaken diagnosis. What better way for doctors to cut an administrator down to size? Okay, so the National Institutes of Health at Bethesda backed up the findings. The experts have been wrong before, especially around Washington, D.C.

Wayne picked me up at the airport and we walked and talked until the early hours of the morning, touching on the dreaded subject briefly. Both of us tried to duck it. In our work we try to help critically ill people, but when it hits home, neither of us is much good.

I felt confused and angry, but also guilty that I should be the one who was spared.

As the story of his illness made the rounds of the hospital, the staff responded to Wayne in amazing ways as he carried out his responsibilities. His doctors marveled at his focus and drive. One of them said that Wayne's room was "more like an office than a sick room. We would unplug him from his IVs so that he could attend meetings and carry on business as usual. The only issue that ever arose between us, as a patient/doctor, was how much he could do. I lost most of these arguments willingly, and it never ceased to amaze me how much drive he had. He showed me the true meaning of a full life."

One of his other doctors said that "the most revealing moments of Wayne's optimism appeared during the final days, when in spite of fever, pain, and the blurring confusion of the technicalities of intensive care, he managed to lie propped up in bed with his felt-tipped pen and yellow note pad and plan for the business of tomorrow. He died as he lived—planning for a new and better day."

THE MONUMENT

Two of Wayne's sons carried a huge flat rock up over 14,000 feet to the top of Mt. Whitney, the highest mountain in the continental United States. They left it there with their father's name, WAYNE, inscribed in large letters across the face of it. Perhaps climbers will come by and carve their own names of a family member or friend on it. Wayne was the kind of guy who would shrug his shoulders and say, "The more the merrier!"

Most of us hope that we will leave some reminder behind; otherwise gravestone makers would soon go out of business. But a personal memorial, the impression we leave with people, is the most enduring kind, one that requires some sacrifice on our part. Aging gives us time to think what kind of monument we can erect for others, and what kind we would like to leave for others to remember us.

ALONE

> My God, my God, why hast thou forsaken me?
>
> MATTHEW 27:46

These dry, gasping words of Jesus are among the most terrifying in history. Worse than dying is dying forsaken by all, especially by the one who is the Center of life. Now that the Center is crumbling, what hope is there? Jesus was left to die alone in the desert like a dog, no longer cared for by his master. But after his cry of dereliction came the surrender, and the resurrection of his faith, "Father, into thy hands I commend my spirit."

At the same time that my daughter Joy graduated from college, my brother Wayne died. He had urged me to go to her graduation, saying, "Don't worry, I'll still be around." But the night before, I saw a young doctor hurry from Wayne's room, shocked and mumbling something like, "He's worse off than we thought." Nevertheless, I went to Joy's graduation.

Wayne died the day my daughter graduated from the University of Oregon.

I could not be in both places at once. Deep down I feared not only Wayne's death, but my own as well. It was far easier to celebrate a graduation than it was to watch Wayne die. Knowing him, I am sure he is smiling and saying, "God and I made it fine without you, Bro. Please don't give it another thought."

A great lover of people, Wayne still had the gift of being alone without being lonely. When no one was around, he read or worked on future plans for the hospital he loved and administered so gracefully.

Thoughts on the Way
to Picking Out a Niche

Surely goodness and mercy shall follow me
all the days of my life;
and I shall dwell in the house of the Lord
forever.

PSALM 23:6

"Bob, we've got to go now," my wife called out, reminding me that we had an appointment at the local cemetery to pick out a double niche in a wall for our "remains." Great.

Someday Gabriel, or whoever determines such matters, will call out like my wife did, and of course, I won't be ready, and I will do everything possible to drag my feet. I have conducted hundreds of funerals, but I will be tight-lipped at my own.

The cemetery office with its computers and plot maps with pins looked like any other real estate office, except that once the tenants move in there are no complaints about loud music or rowdy neighbors. Jim, the young man behind the counter, tried to cheer us up with a wide smile and what is probably his standard greeting, "My, you folks certainly are on time!" Maybe the majority of his customers come late; no use hurrying the matter. While I am sometimes tardy to events, being on time for my funeral will be out of my hands.

I asked Jim if we could just rent a niche; he didn't seem to get the joke, but gave me his professional funeral business smile.

As I rode home next to my lovely wife, I died a small death. Someday, I will travel this same route, but she will maybe follow behind in a gray Caddy, probably chauffeured by the same joker behind the counter. The thought of this final separation is almost more than I can bear. I have great admiration for those who accept the absolute finality of death. While they have more courage than I do, I have hints that tell me that whatever Power brought Muriel and me together will still be in force even after we have been put in our niches in the "Garden of the Oaks." Somehow the Power that created us from dust will recreate us in a form that will defy any fantasy we might have.

I have a hunch that "Amazing Grace" will be sufficient.

No One Can Do It for Us

You got to walk that lonesome valley,
you got to walk it by yourself.
There is no one who can walk it for you;
you've got to walk it for yourself.

AFRICAN AMERICAN SPIRITUAL

Older people are often lonely, particularly when we sense that people no longer wish to hear about our infirmities. And thank God, we come to the conclusion that we no longer have to recite them in lurid detail.

We will all die alone; no one can do it for us. But we can learn to make our loneliness a preparation for the time when the mystery awaits us. If we know that God is at the side of our recliner, we can trust that God will be at our deathbed as well. As we are gently invaded by grace, we sense the "peace which passes all understanding," especially when we find people who trust God now and in eternity. Together we find that God desires nothing so much as to comfort us, to be God for us.

But as much as we need the comfort and experience of others to guide us, there comes a point where we have to journey by ourselves. Friends can point the way, but the travel is ours alone.

Ever-present God, help us to hear you speak
in the words of others, but also help us
to hear you in the solitude we all face now,
and totally when we die.

WHEN JACKIE ROBINSON
VISITED OUR CHURCH

In the summer of 1952, I called the Brooklyn Dodgers office and asked if Jackie Robinson would speak to inner-city youth at the church I served, in Pittsburgh, Pennsylvania. I never stopped to think that if the Dodger star accepted every such invitation, he would never have time to play baseball.

He came early; there were no newspaper reporters or TV people trailing along. This was not a photo op for the Brooklyn Dodgers to show off their MVP, or to win a few points with church folks.

Jackie Robinson talked about loyalty to family, working hard in school and at sports, and above all, trusting in God. He echoed the words of his mother, who had told him, "God will take care of you. You are a child of God, made in God's image. Because God is there, nothing can go wrong with you. You can allow yourself to take risks because you just know that the Lord will not allow you to sink so far that you can't swim."

Words were secondary; what moved us was the presence of this furiously competitive athlete—who many would call America's greatest all-round baseball player, on or off the field—standing up and speaking from his heart.

Glancing at his watch, he said that it was time for him to go to work. Before he left, he asked everyone to join him in something he said every night whether he was on the road or at home. With one hand, he took the hand of a black boy and with the other, the hand of a white boy, and led us in the Lord's Prayer.

As he waved goodbye, his young fans affectionately mobbed him. He tried to shake as many hands as he could before diving into his car. I leaned into the car window for a last goodbye, then with horror saw that his dashing, cream-colored suit bore the handprints of almost every stickball player in the neighborhood.

"Please send us the cleaning bill," I called to him.

"I think that the Dodgers can handle that," he said, smiling.

Navigating this mob was easy compared to the many professional and personal crises Robinson battled before he was called out by a fatal disease. He faced death the way he would steal home, knowing that he could be tagged out, but confident that whatever the score, the effort was worth it.

Jackie died of heart disease and related problems on October 24, 1972. On the day before, he went to his office in Englewood Hills, and afterwards asked his driver to stop at various wholesalers where Robinson collected meat, canned goods, and other food. Then they dropped these off at Lacy Covington's Nazarene Baptist Church for the needy in Brooklyn.

In his tribute, *New York Times* columnist Red Smith wrote: "The word for Jackie

Robinson is 'unconquerable.' He would not be defeated; not by any other team and not by life." Yankee catcher Yogi Berra, in his own inimitable manner, said about Robinson, "He could beat you in a lot of ways."

None of us beat death, but because of Jesus we can steal home. That should give us a Robinson-like courage to face whatever curve balls life throws at us.

A CLASS ACT TO THE END

‐✦‐

> . . . a time to be born, and a time to die. . . .
>
> ECCLESIASTES 3:2

We spent eleven of our last twelve New Year's Eves together—Carolyn and Don, Muriel and me. One day the doctors discovered Carolyn had ovarian cancer, which soon spread throughout her body.

She lost her hair from radiation treatments. Later when it grew back in short silvery curls, women stopped and asked her who her hair stylist was. "You wouldn't want to know," she said, smiling in her sexy way. One friend said, "She was a class act, right to the end."

Almost to the end, she remained hopeful that one of the many treatments she tried would lead to a cure, or at least to a long remission. But it was not to be, and she died quietly at home, surrounded by her family and with a small Cross of St. Francis clutched in her hand.

It wasn't that she made dying seem easy; it's just that she did not want to be a burden on her family and friends.

During the prayers at the memorial service, family and friends were invited to mention aloud some gift that Carolyn had given them. "Loyalty, humor, fun to be with, unselfish, a great mom, a wonderful wife. . . ." This list of gifts exploded around the sanctuary like popcorn.

THE BUICK IN DON'S DELI

If God is for us, who is against us?

ROMANS 8:31

While on a visit to my daughter and grand-children on the Big Island of Hawaii, I sat on a bench to read a newspaper in front of Don's Deli. Don's is an ice-cream spot that appeals to the tourists who come to see King Kamehameha's statue across the street.

Suddenly, I heard the revving of a car engine, and a new Buick Regal shot by me. The problem was that the Buick was not on the street in front of Don's Deli. Instead, it had crashed into the eating area, stopping alongside my bench. Astonishingly, just minutes before, customers had left the table now crushed under the Regal's front wheels. The car was buried so far inside Don's place that the driver could have reached out for a cup of coffee, an unintended drive-in.

Who can I thank for my narrow escape? My lucky stars? God? I have long lived on borrowed time. An advantage of surviving many dangers, toils, and snares is that the future holds less terror than it once did. My hope for tomorrow is based upon the myriad ways God has been with me today.

After 9/11, every time we read the newspaper or turn on the television, the whole world needs the reassurance that Jesus has been there. He knew the end was near when he heard the clanging of Roman armor. For us, it could be the revving of a Buick engine.

DEADLINE

... our Savior Christ Jesus, who abolished death
and brought life and immortality to light. ...

2 TIMOTHY 1:10

One of my teachers thought that death was
a terrible waste of human talent. But without death, the world would soon be overrun
with talented people, and some not so talented. Death is the great equalizer; no one is
exempt.

There is nothing more democratic than
death. The President of the United States and
the homeless person are the same at death,
no matter the splendor of the funeral or the
price of the casket.

Supposing we lived for eons, would we
make the best use of our talents if we knew
that we had all the time in the world? Death

stares us in the face and we are reminded with each passing friend that our turn will come all too soon.

There are so many books to read, maybe a few to write, and so little time. When I was a reporter, I worked on deadlines and found that I needed them or I could dawdle all day on a piece. No pun intended, but there is a deadline facing each of us. We still have time to tell some special people that we love them and thank them for things they have done for us. I wish I had thanked my mother again in later years for staying up all night and sewing a pup tent for me, and for so much else she did. We still have time to tell some people that we are sorry for the hurtful things we said or did. In some cases, the best thing may be to treat those people with love and kindness, and forget the past.

THE HOME STRETCH

Lord, you pick 'em up, and I'll put 'em down.

A RUNNER'S PRAYER

As an undergraduate at the University of Minnesota, I ran the mile and two mile on the track team. I was never a fast runner, so I hoped to prevail through endurance and sheer stubbornness. The problem was that even if I kept up with the pack for most of the race, the fast ones beat me in the home stretch. Others knew better than I when to start their finishing kick.

Coming into the last turn I would start my sprint, but I never got the timing quite right. I would start too soon and pull ahead of the pack, only to fade in the last few yards as wiser runners conserved their energy for the final burst. Or, I would wait too long, only to hit the finishing line with an unspent reserve, and hardly a winner. If only I could have timed it right, I might have become a fair runner, despite a lack of talent.

What we do on the home stretch often says more than what we do at any other time. The finish often matters most. But our human nature is to postpone any consideration of the end, to think that the finish line is a long way off.

Nearing the end, we struggle to unload the baggage that slows us down. We find that we can improve a bit with age; we learn to unload more gracefully and finish better than we started. We have been running for a long time, and maybe we still have not perfected the timing of our kick; but we know more about how to finish than we did years ago. We know that we must make this race count above others, and we intend to make it our best race. The fact that it may come near the end of our racing days adds excitement, even joy, to it. Because it comes late in life, we are ready to unload all the baggage and go all out!

If our legs and our lungs are not what they once were, we'll make up for it with our hearts. There is no holding back now as we prepare to give our last and best race all that we have!

> . . . let us also lay aside every weight,
>   and sin which clings so closely,
>   and let us run with perseverance
>   the race that is set before us. . . .

HEBREWS 12:1

KAY AND LEE

Kay had crippling arthritis for many years, spending her last ones in a wheelchair. People with all types of illnesses and handicaps rallied around her as their patron saint. With Kay's enthusiastic leadership, Prayer House in Tucson, Arizona was established for people of all faiths who desired to pray with others more than on Saturday or Sunday. But except for a few brief remissions, her knotted and twisted body never got better. People often asked her how she felt when others, but not her, were healed. She would reply that there were two kinds of healing—one of the spirit and one of the body. "I received the first and best one, and I haven't given up on receiving the second. Besides, in Tucson I don't have to worry about slipping on the ice."

The other member in this partnership of saints, a designation he would most assuredly deny, was husband Lee, the faithful spouse and friend with the husky voice, the quick, soft laugh, the steady hand at Kay's elbow. The way in which they managed their suffering is what turned it from a cross to a crown. They drew great strength from the lonely, misunderstood carpenter-prophet as he trudged ahead of them stumbling with his cross, then picking it up again. Not simply "take up your cross," for Kay and Lee, but take it up and "follow me." Jesus' cross was not so much in the weight and pain of it, but in the way he used it as the loftiest pulpit in human history.

Surely Jesus recently greeted Kay with the words, "Well done, good and faithful servant; you have been faithful over a little, I will set you over much; enter into the joy of your master" (Matt. 25:21).

The full circle of those words of Jesus is one of the best reasons to believe that death does not end life. Because Kay and Lee experienced that God had already defeated the death of the spirit in this life, they knew that God had abolished it forever.

Maybe God Is a Work in Progress

President Roosevelt's hearty reassurance "The only thing we have to fear is fear itself" seems naïve today. Chicken Little's "The sky is falling" seems more appropriate.

Many of our fears have to do with losing control over our physical, even our spiritual, lives. Extremists have the debatable advantage of receiving clear-cut directions from their God, while others of us muddle through with free will and the mystery of God.

Rather than removing or overcoming fear, God enters into the smoldering pile with us. God's heart was the first to break when the Twin Towers came cascading down. God knew the terror in the hearts of the one-way passengers, and heard the pleas for mercy even God could not answer, granting instead the vast freedom God gives us.

We may discover that true faith is not restricted to certain religions, but is a universal, holy gift given to those whose hearts are open. Good and true religion is that which makes us more loving. Like the manna in the wilderness, faith comes to us one day at a time, as we need it. We cannot imagine the extent of faith needed to live just today and tomorrow amid all the terror of our world.

Gentle, faithful people believe that no matter what happens in this life, God will be there in the best and worst of times.

God is our refuge and strength,
 a very present help in trouble.
Therefore we will not fear though
 the earth should change,
though the mountains shake
 in the heart of the sea. . . .

Psalm 46:1–2

When Jesus said goodbye to his disciples, he knew that some of them would probably suffer torture and death as he would. He knew that their hearts were gripped with the same fear that gripped his. Unable to offer them an easy way out, his last words to them were words of presence and hope. He told them he would be with them always, in this life and beyond.

Don't Worry, Pastor, I Know Where I'm Going!

It's too bad dying is the last thing we do; it teaches us so much about living.

"Mrs. T," as she was known in the neighborhood, was born into a black sharecropper's family in Mississippi and moved north as a young girl. For over twenty years she cleaned the homes of affluent white people in the suburbs of Chicago, often traveling by bus for an hour and a half to work. After she was stricken with cancer, she still continued to work as the sole support of Sally, her lively 12-year-old daughter.

Sally became part of our youth group and brought her mother to worship every Sunday. When Mrs. T became too sick to attend, she sent her daughter with a little envelope containing one dollar, a generous gift from a poor woman.

Even this intrepid woman could not hold out too long. Soon she lay dying, a little bag of gray bones in the fifty-bed charity ward of the Cook County Hospital. I located her by spotting a picture of Jesus and a lithograph of the church at her bedside. When she saw that I was shocked at how fast she had deteriorated in two days, she extended her two pipe-stem arms, took my hand and comforted me: "Don't worry, Pastor, I know where I'm going!"

Like Jesus, Mrs. T knew that she had come from God and was going to God (John 13:3). Grace filled every inch of her cot in the hot, smelly ward. Her simple trust in God taught me more than any seminary class. I don't remember what I said or prayed, but guess who ministered to whom? Sometimes when I am discouraged, I think of Mrs. T and the gutsy, faithful way she faced the end of her journey. She was a Spirit-filled woman who went ahead, lighting the way for the rest of us.

How Can I Ever Forgive
That Person?

... and should not you have had mercy on
your fellow servant, as I had mercy on you?

MATTHEW 18:33

Forgiveness is a tricky business. We pray,
"Forgive us our sins as we forgive those who
sin against us," yet we hope that God will be
more generous with us than we are with each
other. But some people keep hurting us over
and over again and we find it hard to keep forgiving them. One woman said that her sister
treats her like their abusive mother did; and
every time she is with her sister, the wounds
caused by their mother are reopened. She
loves both of them, but does not like them.
It took her almost a lifetime to discover that
she could love someone she often disliked.

Whatever the circumstances, we discover that we need to forgive others for the sake of our own emotional health. "It's too much work to get up every morning hating so and so," one man said about a politician he despised.

Often there is unfinished forgiveness near the end of life. How can we forgive? First, we can vow never to try to get even with the person who has hurt us; revenge helps neither of us. Second, we can pray for that person—praying for someone soothes the hurt and lubricates forgiveness. Jesus prayed from the cross, "Father, forgive them; for they know not what they do" (Luke 23:34).

Continuing to hate the person we are praying for is like trying to light a candle in a rainstorm.

LEARNING THE SCALES FIRST

———

We learn to pray by learning our prayers. Even "Now I lay me down to sleep; I pray the Lord my soul to keep . . ." is a good place to begin. That childhood prayer taught many of us that God is with us whether we are awake or asleep, and that our final resting place is with God. Then we graduated to other prayers like the Lord's Prayer, given by Jesus to his disciples as an example of how they ought to pray. "Pray then like this," he told them. "Our Father who art in heaven . . ." (Matthew 6:9).

Serious musicians first learn the scales and how to read music. Many of them also learn the principles of classical music and how to perform, or at least to appreciate, a church anthem or a symphony. After they have learned the basics, they can improvise. Benny Goodman and Duke Ellington were at home with swing or Stravinsky. Frank Lloyd Wright was trained in classical architecture before he went on to develop his own distinctive style. Writers must learn the rules of grammar and the logic of an essay before they can forget the rules and write offbeat prose or soaring poetry. Otherwise they are only typing, as one critic said.

Before prayer can become as natural as breathing, we must struggle with the prayers of believers who have gone ahead of us. The literature of the church is filled with prayers for each Sunday and collects for a wide variety of occasions. We learn how to pray without ceasing as we learn St. Francis' prayer: "Lord, make me an instrument of your peace. Where there is hatred, let me sow love. . . ."

We never outgrow our need for set prayers, as we also often pray in free and unstructured ways. Written prayers are the piled-up wisdom of those who have conversed with the Holy before us. Our own prayers are deepened and made more powerful as we read and pray the prayers of others.

Many of us read structured prayers, and pray them in worship and on other occasions, but often our prayers get mixed together with all that is going on around and inside us. Someone asks us to pray for them or for someone dear to them, and we gladly agree. But our very agreement to pray is already a prayer; we pray before we can form the words on our lips. It's like breathing in and breathing out; it becomes second nature for us. Prayer is not a virtue; it is a necessity. How can we talk about the virtue of breathing?

Prayer without ceasing is more about an inner attitude than it is about audible words. The difference between remembering someone in prayer and just remembering them is that in prayer we hold the person up before God, or we try to see them as God sees them. We remember someone, not to get even with that person, but we remember to leave him or her in God's hands.

Prayer is seeing others as God sees them. We grow restless with how slowly the mills of justice grind, and how many criminals are released back on the streets. We might even like to take the law into our own hands and give them what they deserve. When we are instructed by Jesus to pray for our enemies, it is as much for our sake as it is for our enemies'. We pray for our enemies so that they might not drag us down into the bottomless pit of hate.

When we pray without ceasing, we begin to read the newspaper and watch newscasts with new eyes and new ears. As we read about a young ex-convict who says that his most satisfying job as a prisoner was throwing sandbags to save towns from a raging flood, we pray to God that this willing young man will find work on the outside. "I've worked 18 hours a day for $3.00 a week. I'm a hard worker; I'll start at the bottom. Making $3.00 an hour would be a big accomplishment for me," he said.

In his letter to the Romans, Paul speaks of prayer as sometimes a wordless dialogue with God. "For we do not know how to pray as we ought, but the Spirit . . . intercedes for us with sighs too deep for words" (Romans 8:26). If prayer is sighing heavenward, many of us do more praying than we think!

My prayers are selfish. I pray earnestly for my own needs, but my sin pervades even my prayers, perhaps especially my prayers. I know that prayer should ultimately be about doing God's will, not about asking God to do my will. Hopefully, my wishes may yet bend to God's wishes.

Instead of human possibilities, we can celebrate the unimagined possibilities of God. We don't need proof that God answers prayer so much as we need people like Jesus who prayed "great drops of blood" (Luke 22:44).

If politics is the art of the possible, then prayer must be the art of the impossible.

BEFORE IT'S TOO LATE

And he made from one every nation of [humans]
to live on all the face of the earth. . . .

ACTS 17:26

All of us, if we are honest, have prejudices,
whether it is skin color, weight, socio-
economic status, or gender. The truth is that
all of us have features we were born with
that someone doesn't like; they may even
be jealous of our supposed intelligence. We
forget that there are many forms of intelligence, like poetic or other artistic intelligence, that may not show up on a standard
IQ test.

Maybe it is easier to put aside our prejudices about people's preference and appearance
when we do not look so wonderful ourselves.
It is hard to walk down a hospital corridor

with a silly gown tied in the back and worry about someone else's weight problem.

If we don't like brown or black skins, we need to be prepared to be greeted by a brown-skinned Jesus who looked like other dwellers in the desert.

Help me to see your image in all people.

A Gift for an Older Person

The way of a fool is right in his own eyes,
but a wise man listens to advice.

PROVERBS 12:15

One of the most helpful things people can do for us older and/or sick people is to sit quietly with us and ask: "Grandma, tell me about life when you were a little girl. How has life changed since then? What was better and what was worse about the old days?"

The gift of listening or caring enough to hear an older person's story is often the best present a younger person can bring. We are both enriched by the experience. Maybe, we might like you to make an audio recording of the experience.

Sick people are not only sick of being sick, but life takes on a gray or shadowy look for us. But when we can talk to a sympathetic friend, life becomes less burdensome. Yes, it must be difficult to listen to someone talk about their worries, or pains, particularly if the listener has heard it several times before. But active listening includes gently changing the subject to: "How would you improve the delivery of medical care if you could? What would you say was your greatest accomplishment? Who were some of the most unusual characters you ever met?"

Divine Listener, give us all the gift of listening patiently.

WHERE DO WE FIND PEOPLE
WITH HOPE?

Take from our souls the strain and stress,
And let our ordered lives confess
The beauty of thy peace.

JOHN G. WHITTIER

Many Christians feel that the church is mostly safe and staid. Years ago there was also some concern that God might be dead, but we realized, like Mark Twain, that the announcement of death was highly exaggerated.

The church is made up of human beings, so naturally it is all-too-human itself. But it is also the coming together of broken and sinful people who constantly need to hear the Good News: that God loves sinners and sent Jesus to change our hearts, even to die if that's what it takes.

But do we need the church? Do we need to belong to some group, which too often is concerned with saving itself? When the question becomes one of the survival of the church, that isn't much of an exciting reason for people to rally around.

But if the question is how I personally face my own death with hope, that becomes a different matter. Then I need to be reminded of others who have traveled ahead of me and met their death with a hope that was beyond them.

People who courageously and peacefully face death, even relatively so, have a secret to pass on to the rest of us who will die. What is the source of their brave, personal philosophy? What about those of us who are not very brave?

I remember my father, just before he died, saying that the sheets had been changed, the pastor has brought him the Holy Communion, and he was ready to go now.

WHO KNOWS WHAT I MIGHT BE?

And Jesus said, "Neither do I condemn you;
go, and do not sin again."

JOHN 8:11

Maybe I'm crazier than most people, but I often regret my mistakes and sins of the past. I know that I cannot undo these, and I know that God and most people have forgiven me. Still, there is one person who will not forgive me. Me.

I suppose that not forgiving myself, after God has forgiven me, may be the "unforgivable sin." So now I have one more blasted thing to feel badly about. When most of my body feels miserable, my heart and mind follow.

But there is hope. God uses my mistakes and misdeeds to bring about something good. Things I regret have broken my hard shell so that grace can find its own way into me. Otherwise, I would go blissfully along, not worrying much about what I say or do.

Some people think that old age gives us license to speak our minds, "to tell it like it is." Okay, but when is it simply an excuse for being rude?

Maybe feeling guilty about the past has its good side; I may be a little more careful about what I do and say today.

All my regrets cannot change the past.
Help me to trust your forgiveness instead.

THE KISS OF DEATH

Death is swallowed up in victory.

1 CORINTHIANS 15:54

St. Francis called it "Sister Death," alien words in this day of fighting off death as long as possible, and then deep-freezing the corpse. "Come, sweet death" is, similarly, a rarely heard invitation. Still, death is now stubbornly being dragged out of the closet, despite the efforts of morticians and others to deny it.

Charlie died on a vacation in Hawaii, and the undertaker in Minnesota made him look so lifelike that his friends remarked: "Doesn't old Charlie look great? That trip to Hawaii sure did him a world of good, didn't it?"

Among the thousands of critically ill

people I have called upon, only a handful said they wished for death. Most hoped for a cure; others awaited death with a stoic faith, while a few agreed with Dylan Thomas: "Do not go gentle into that good night./ Rage, rage against the dying of the light." The latter seems at odds with the belief that we are going to a better place. In the meantime, many of us do our best to keep the medical profession thriving and the drug manufacturers rich.

While we may not become buddies with death, there comes a time when all of us are forced to surrender to the inevitable. Maybe we begin by seeing death as a line in the sand that marks the end of our existence as we know it. This knowledge may push us into doing some things we have long postponed. What do we do when time is running out on us? Is there likely to be a better time to deal with our death than right now?

I am inspired by the faith of an 82-year-old friend who has suffered from crippling poliomyelitis since he was 16, a long life, particularly for a victim of polio. When he reached 75, he said that his body had already died and that he was running purely on spirit. I cannot say this myself, but I pray for some of the grace he has found.

THE FAITH OF TWO OLD MEN

I called an old buddy with whom I marched from Selma to Montgomery in the days of Martin Luther King, Jr. A former priest and a retired psychologist, Ed is always good for a few laughs; next to prayer, it's the best therapy I know.

We told some medical war stories and some lies, and agreed that we are both fine except that our bodies are falling apart. Our old cars are in better shape than we are.

My friend, who had one foot out the door of the priesthood when we traveled to Selma, said he was now an atheist. Then he made his "confession of faith," which was a bitter condemnation of all institutionalized religion, except that he goes all the way to say there is no God. I agreed with many of his complaints about the church, Protestant or Catholic, but said that he was throwing the baby out with the bath water. "What if there is no 'baby'?" he replied. We ended the conversation agreeing that both our cases rested upon faith.

Becoming an atheist is a reasonable response to the history and corruption of institutional religion, but our faith is in God, not in a fallible church, which both portrays and betrays God. My small boat of faith still manages to ride the waves and the battering that come to us all. Despite sharing some of Ed's questions, I cannot imagine life without God; I don't have enough faith to be an atheist. My friend has nevertheless gone beyond doubt to a certainty about the non-being of God. If I am wrong, I have still had a good life, and so has he. I don't believe that God measures out divine love in the same parsimonious (and sanctimonious!) way we do.

My friend cares about people, and for years he listened to tales of woe that others would find insufferable. Many of his clients went away feeling that somehow life was worthwhile. He serves as a reminder that many of us Christians could do a much better job of showing, not just telling, our faith. There are no arguments that will change either of our positions. All we can do is to continue to care and let God, or whatever gives us hope and joy, work it out.

CURIOSITY

And this is eternal life, that they know thee
the only true God, and Jesus Christ,
whom thou hast sent.

JOHN 17:3

A hospice pastor who calls upon many sick
and dying patients said that people seldom
ask him about heaven. He notes that most
people worry about how their family will be,
whether their will is done properly, or similar
concerns.

If any of us were taking a trip to a foreign
country we had never visited, wouldn't we
be curious about what to expect? What is life
like there? Will I see my loved ones?

It seems strange that people going on an
eternal journey should express little curios-
ity about their destination. Do you ever think

about heaven? What would you ask your pastor or spiritual guide, without expecting her to be a celestial travel agent? What would you say if you were the hospice pastor that would be both honest and helpful?

Maybe the whole question has to be rephrased: "Are there words even to ask the question about the mystery that awaits us?" It may be enough to say again with Paul: ". . . whether we live or whether we die, we are the Lord's" (Romans 14:8).

Jesus, you didn't give us much information about heaven except that "in my Father's house are many rooms. . . . I go to prepare a place for you." Best of all, you said: "Because I live, you will live also" (John 14:2, 19).

Help!

More things are wrought by prayer
than the world dreams of.

ALFRED LORD TENNYSON

If I had to sum up prayer in one word, it
would be "help!"—help in an infinite number of ways. Help to be more an instrument of
God than a burden to others; help me to live
with my physical disabilities without recit-
ing them to others; help with my mercurial
faith; help with my selfish love; help with
hope for the future. Help! Help! Help!

Breathe on me, breath of God;
Fill me with life anew,
That I may love all that you love,
And do what you would do.

EDWIN HATCH

THE LAST WORD

None of us lives to himself,
and none of us dies to himself. . . .
Whether we live or whether we die,
we are the Lord's.

ROMANS 14:7–8

He was a devoted and learned Catholic priest who taught theology in a nearby seminary. We had many lunches together, during which I defended the Catholic Church and he defended the Lutheran Church.

Once we got into a very personal discussion about life after death. Since both of us were in our seventies, with the usual afflictions that come with that age, we had some stake in the matter. We agreed that a heaven of harps and pie in the sky did not sound very appealing, not forever, anyway.

We talked about how unjust this life is for so many millions of people. We had both visited dirt-poor people in slums in the U.S. and in Mexico. How must God feel when little children starve to death or are burned by bombs? Both of us had ministered to good people who suffered greatly, and to some not so good who prospered well. It was hard to believe that God has a bias toward the poor, as some people say.

We decided that heaven must be where God's final justice is accomplished. After all the bloodied games of human history, there must be a game where God bats cleanup.

If injustice and death have the last word, there is no hope for us, but we both bet our lives that in Jesus Christ, God has the last word.

I believe; help my unbelief!

MARK 9:24

GRATITUDE

O Lord my God,
I will give thanks to thee forever.

PSALM 30:12

A common problem with inherited money is that the inheritors seldom realize its value because they did not have to work for it. Have you ever given someone something of value, only to have him or her treat it as though it were of no value, like a handmade oak table they left to weather in the patio?

Maybe God feels this way about the way we treat the gifts of our lives and the beautiful earth we live upon. We complain about the injustice of life, and about its brevity, while we spend hours fussing over our car or pouring quarters in a slot machine.

When we think of sin we often conjure up

images of black lingerie and bottles of booze, which have sabotaged more than one life. But a more common sin that we succumb to is failing to appreciate the life God has given us. Instead of rejoicing in what we have and who we are, we cast jealous eyes about us.

Stop and think: Would we really like to trade our lot with that of anyone else? Those who win millions in the lottery or in a mind-boggling TV show often have a short and un-happy time with their prize.

If we could put all of our troubles and joys in a bag, and everyone cast their bag in a ring, chances are we would take our own bag back. Part of the good news is that there is still time to take it back.

God, please grant each of us the gift of gratitude.

MURIEL

The pact of love is eternity's beginning in time.

SØREN KIERKEGAARD

Even more than giving us a comforting companion on earth, marriage helps prepare us for the fullness of God's love. As we learn to love and forgive each other now, our souls are being forged to last forever. Of all of God's blessings, the gift of a loving partner is the greatest one of all.

Our deepest spiritual struggle is learning to become more gentle and considerate of our mate. Some women complain that their husbands never tell them that they love them. Sometimes a man will reveal his love in so many ways, that she need not wonder. But a few gracious words from the strong silent type would help.

Some of us feel free to express our anger at home more than at work, when the latter may be the source of our frustration. Proverbs says, "He who is slow to anger is better than the mighty, and he who rules his spirit than he who takes a city." Any city.

Jesus said that in marriage, we become "one flesh." Besides the delight of the physical, one flesh means that we care as much about our partner's hopes and dreams as we care about our own. The difference between continuing a work or abandoning it may be a few words of appreciation from the person who means the most to us. More than once, Muriel's encouragement has kept me from tossing everything aside, and kicking tires at a car lot.

A marriage or deep friendship provides incubation for creativity.

Many authors cite a spouse or a partner as the one most responsible for the completion of their work. In a good marriage, we do not have to spend precious time looking for support. If there were no Grandpa Moses,

Grandma Moses would have needed someone else who believed that she could paint in earnest, beginning at age 75!

Marriage can be life's greatest joy and life's greatest sorrow. To lose someone upon whom we have depended for most of our life can be the most staggering blow there is. The better the relationship, the deeper the sorrow. Often we cannot help but become too dependent upon our partner, even to making him or her a God-substitute. Fortunately, God is not jealous in the same way that we are jealous, and seems to overlook our humanity.

God blesses us in our solitude, but often God more than doubles the blessings in a marriage or a partnership.

DEFUSING

It is worth repeating:

> He who is slow to anger is better than
> the mighty, and he who rules his spirit
> than he who takes a city.

PROVERBS 16:32

Usually when I complain or get cranky, my wife listens, then quietly acknowledges whatever legitimacy my case has. Rarely does she answer crankiness with crankiness, or anger with anger, saving us many a useless argument. I hope that I occasionally do some of the defusing, but her good humor makes me want to apologize for my bad humor. The result, from my perspective at least, is that after fifty-five years our marriage gets even better.

With road rage and all types of personal grievances, no friendship, or even community, could long endure without defusers. And as we age and/or become ill, we are increasingly in need of defusing. When our darker moods strike us, it helps to turn to those friends who can allow us to talk ourselves down without judging us. Such friends are rare and we are well advised to use them sparingly. Hopefully we are also good listeners, bringing equity and deep bonding to the relationship.

The movie *Grumpy Old Men* was a comic portrayal of an almost universal condition. Few of us escape becoming old curmudgeons in one way or another. Sometimes the young receptionist in the doctor's office, or even the doctor or nurse, is already too harassed and not as sympathetic as we would like. A physically handicapped friend of mine makes it a point to treat medical and restaurant people with tender loving care, sometimes laying it on a bit thick, but better this than complaining. His ability to schmooze with them

makes him a welcome sight as he drives his
electric scooter into the room.

God, soothe our fevered brows
and help us to grow old gracefully.

OVER FIFTY YEARS

Pettiness answered with patience,
Testiness with tenderness,
Fifty years my indulgent bride:
God's gift, well wrapped.

'32 Chevy convertible. Red.
Squeaky brakes, deaf father.
Hormones racing,
Idling for theology and politics.

Quiet girl met motor-mouth:
Mysteries of God
Solved over a nickel coke.
Grace without limits.

RICHARD

Richard and I consider ourselves blessed far beyond our deserving with beautiful, strong, loving wives. But sometimes men talk frankly with each other in different ways than a man and a woman talk, even in the best of marriages.

We were classmates at a Lutheran seminary in Minneapolis over fifty years ago. We knew each other by name only, since he lived in the single men's dorm and I lived off campus with my wife and two children.

After graduation, Richard organized three churches in Texas and I served inner-city churches in Pittsburgh and Chicago. He was a shy young man who had to muster all his courage to knock on the doors of strangers, the vast majority of whom had never before set foot inside a Lutheran church. Since he had a deep interest in science as well as theology, he attracted more men prospects than women. Sturdy and muscular, he now wears fatigues like the camper and mountain climber he still is.

Richard and three other classmates held a mini-reunion in Las Vegas on September 11, 2001. The rest of our class who were well enough to travel had our flight reservations canceled. Later Richard and I began face-to-face meetings as a two-man reunion. In less than three years, we have talked and, more importantly, listened, to each other several times from morning to night. No TV, radio, or newspapers, just opening our emotional and spiritual sides to each other. We both are as honest and caring as we can be.

We soon discovered that neither of us believed in a God who barbecues people in hell. Richard says that he is an atheist, which I can understand after his trying to convert Texans into Lutherans. After that, he spent over thirty years teaching science in the Riverside Community College in southern California, while I had itchy feet and served several churches across the country, ending in Palo Alto, California.

So far in eight meetings, the discussion always drifts to a subject most everyone avoids talking about: Death. Richard seems at peace with the idea that his body will simply return to the dust it came from, and there will be no more Richard again. Ever. As I have said, I do not have enough faith to be an atheist. We know that both theism and atheism leave unanswered questions, such as "How did we get here?" and more significantly, "Why?" and "Why is evil so powerful?"

I believe that the Power that created us still remembers us after we die; that, as St. Paul said, "Whether we live or whether we die, we are the Lord's." Neither Richard nor I can prove our "faith," but I think that Richard still loves the God he doesn't believe in, as one sage once remarked.

IS THERE HOPE FOR ME?

Risen Lord, all human hopes are finally dashed.
Overcome our lingering doubts and help us
hold on to your promise. . . .
"Because I live, you shall live also."

JOHN 14:19

I asked a group of elderly people what Easter meant to them. "Hope," said one woman.

The hope of Easter is different from any other of our hopes. People once hoped that World War I would make the world safe for democracy. But today the world is still insanely engaged in an arms race and a war, which make it unsafe for everyone. We put our hope in friends, only to have some of them misunderstand us. Or we hope that we will always have good health and avoid suffering; but we know that is a vain hope. Even if we live to be 100, we know that all life ends in death.

The hope of Easter begins where all other hopes leave off. From beginning to end, Easter is the work of God alone. No one really expected Jesus' resurrection: the women who came to the tomb were surprised and frightened, the disciples fled, and Thomas doubted. Later they believed, and some of them died rather than deny their hope, their Lord.

A MAN OF SORROWS

You will be sorrowful,
but your sorrow will turn into joy.

JOHN 16:20

Isaiah prophesied that Jesus would be "a man of sorrows and acquainted with grief." This should be a comfort to all of us who, despite our faith, sometimes feel sad and lonely. "No one knows the sorrows I've seen," the old spiritual says.

Often we don't know specifically what it is that makes us sad, but we have a sense that all is not right with the world, or at least, all is not right with us.

An understanding friend, exercise, a compassionate pastor, doctor, or psychologist, and a good book can give us a lift, but the sadness often returns. We can phone a sick person, or best of all, get out of the house and visit someone who is hurting. There are no pat answers for our sadness. It helps to accept the fact that most sadness is part of life, just as joy and satisfaction are. Often, a listening friend and prayer are the best healers of all. Because Jesus knew sorrow, he can help us with ours.

How Do You Say Goodbye to Your Father?

Forgive us our debts,
As we also have forgiven our debtors. . . .

MATTHEW 6:12

My father was a verbally abusive man and said things that he surely regretted. Despite his harsh words, I wish that I had been able to say something to him when he died. I wish that it had not taken me so many years to forgive him.

When I last saw him, his six-foot, 185-pound frame had shrunk to less than ninety pounds, a gray skeleton, the size of a young boy. I reached out to touch him as he tried to rasp a few words. Finally, he said "Goodbye, Bob," I replied, "Goodbye, Dad." I wish that both of us had been able to say the three most healing words in the English language, "I love you."

I would say those words to him now, because I found that I needed to forgive him for my sake as much as for his, maybe more so. In order to forgive him, I did not need to like what he said or even like him in some ways. Jesus called upon us to love and forgive those who abuse us, not necessarily to like them. I know that my father loved me in his own peculiar way.

What we would like to say to someone before they die, we could say now while we still have a chance. First, we have to admit that we also regularly hurt the feelings of those we love the most, and also hope for their forgiveness.

STILL TIME

For everything there is a season,
and a time for every matter under heaven.

Our human nature is to postpone any consideration of death until the very end—ask any cemetery lot salesperson. We think that there is always time to do what we intend to do.

It can be any number of "tomorrow things." There is still time to get my work published, and I don't want to depart until I have something to leave for grandchildren, whether they will read it or not. Everyone ought to leave a little remembrance of him- or herself behind. Plant an apple tree or write a poem; it need not even rhyme. The sooner the better.

Do it today, literally for God's sake. Someday soon there will not be a tomorrow. Most of us will die leaving much left to be done. We need grace to do what we can, and forgiveness for what we leave undone.

Maybe when I'm gone someone will put a little flower at my marker with a sign saying: "Late bloomer."

A FORETASTE OF THE
FEAST TO COME

O taste and see that the Lord is good!

PSALM 34:8

A young woman wished to impress a young man and invited him to dinner. She was not an accomplished cook, only she didn't know it. She burned the steak, but thought that special sauce would cover it up. Also, the vegetables were overcooked and soggy. The meal was a near-disaster, but the man bravely ate it. After dessert and coffee, she leaned over and asked, "Did you like it?"

"Yes, it was delicious," he lied, wishing he could ask for a little baking soda.

She came over, sat on his lap, mussed his hair, and cooed: "Just think, when we're married I can cook all of your meals forever."

In the movie *Babette's Feast,* a servant woman in Denmark, who was really a renowned chef in hiding from civil war in France, won 10,000 francs and used the entire amount to prepare a marvelous banquet for the other poor peasants in her village. It was the grandest feast any of them had ever known, as Babette spared neither time nor money, and it brought unimagined joy to their otherwise drab lives.

When we taste of the Lord, we want the feast never to end, the dance never to stop.

THE RED LIGHT

If thou, O Lord, shouldst mark iniquities,
Lord, who could stand?

PSALM 130:3

I burned out my car engine because the red overheating light on the dashboard either didn't come on, or I missed seeing it. (Guess which explanation I gave my wife!) God also warns us like the red light; it's called guilt, but often we keep driving.

The older we get, the more we should be able to recognize the light. God doesn't stop the engine in time for us, but God gives us a warning device—an uneasy conscience.

The best antidote to guilt and punishing ourselves is the good news that God in Jesus forgives sinners. "Just as I am without one plea," we sing. There is nothing we can do to receive the gift; God accepts us totally and freely. Then we have the basis for accepting people of color, gays and lesbians, fat or poor people, and sinners like ourselves.

As we age, it is nice to "mellow." We need not be hard on ourselves or on each other, because by grace God forgives and overlooks all of our sins, every single one of them.

LUNCH AT THE NUT TREE

Two bearded old preachers raced their wheel-chairs at each other at breakneck speed, one on the top and the other at the bottom of a restaurant entrance ramp. Only an expert wheelie by Will, the operator of the motorized chair, avoided a head-on collision. Two proper-looking ladies gasped in horror.

"Don't you call me a washed-up old Bible thumper!" shouted Will, trying to overturn Gil's hand-powered machine.

"I will if I want to . . . out of my way, you old geezer!" cried Gil, his speech impaired.

"Look at us, we're just old kooks, ready for the grave!" Will said, as they high-fived from their circling chairs. The proper ladies turned away in disgust.

After ordering lunch, the talk resumed where it had left off thirty years ago when we met weekly for lunch, only now it was about pensions instead of paychecks, and prostates instead of programs. Gil's wife, Pat, and I settled back as the demolition derby drivers had at each other. The verbal trashing covered up some serious things, but not all of them.

After working as a teaching nun for twenty-five years, Pat met and married Gil. Since his stroke a few years ago, she has taken care of him with religious devotion. "Where do you draw your strength from, Pat?" Will asked, as if he were inquiring about her shrimp salad.

Pat hesitated. "We have each other."

"What are you going to do after Gil goes?" Will asked. I wanted to kick Will's wheelchair, but I was afraid I would set off the demolition derby again.

Pat drew a deep breath. "I'll face that when it comes." Then she added wistfully, "I don't believe what I used to . . . but if it's true, it would be nice."

"I got my doubts too, Pat, but I still believe . . . I can't help myself," Will said, his deep African American spirit reasserting itself.

I tried to separate myself from these handi-capped old men, but someday soon, I would be sitting where they are.

We left promising to see each other again on Martin Luther King's birthday. We agreed it was too bad we didn't live closer; we could use those weekly lunches more than ever.

There we were, three retired preachers and a nun, growing old, trying to comfort each other as we had once comforted the flock. And despite our fears and doubts, we were finding that there was something to the faith we preached after all.

WHAT IF IT ISN'T
GOOD ENOUGH FOR GOD?

O God, our help in ages past,
Our hope for years to come.

ISAAC WATTS

She is an internationally known theologian who was lecturing before a well-educated audience. There was a question about life after death and what it might be like. She replied that traditional ideas of immortality are influenced by Western individualism. She said that her ego didn't need to go on forever, and that "it is okay with me to be just a drop in a vast ocean."

The audience included many senior people, and I could not help but ask her, "Maybe it's okay with you to be a drop in the ocean, but what if it isn't okay with God?"

What if life after death does not have so much to do with self-importance as it does with the completion of God's creation? What if the business of God is not completed with the earthly death of God's creatures? What if all of this leads to something far beyond what any of us can imagine? What if God is a God with an unfinished agenda when we die? What if God does not let go of any of us, not because we are necessary to God, or so interesting to keep around forever, but simply because God loves us, and being a drop in the bucket or the ocean doesn't satisfy the Almighty?

What if God is not playing a cosmic joke, but preparing us for a life beyond our wildest imagination?

FEAR OF REJECTION

With [humans] this is impossible,
but with God all things are possible.

MATTHEW 19:26

Fear is a major barrier to growing from the
pain we encounter. The fear of further rejection and the fear of failure keep many of us
from even trying. The first and most important job of a swim teacher is to help the beginner not to fear the water—to show him
that his body has natural buoyancy which
will keep him afloat with little effort. Once a
person has discovered that, the beginner will
soon learn to swim. But a few of them hug
the edge of the pool, painfully afraid. With
reassurance and coaxing, most of them overcome the fear of failure, take the risk, and
splash into the water.

Few artists would have ever started if they waited until they were certain that the critics would like their work. Writers like Jack London received hundreds of rejections before their work was finally accepted, and Vincent Van Gogh sold only one painting in his lifetime, and that for a hundred dollars, perhaps purchased by his brother Theo, or by someone else who felt sorry for him.

Fear, even more than lack of talent, keeps most of us grounded. We are so afraid of rejection that we never try. For every person who is working on a dream, there are probably four who are still shopping around for the right software.

Jesus knew rejection and did not let it stop him from completing his mission. By grace, we can do the same.

A WORD OF THANKS

A group of friends gathered under the oak trees near the Federal Prison Camp at Lompoc, California. We talked and prayed with an elderly man who was about to serve a year in prison. The unusual part of this story is that Charlie Liteky had won the Congressional Medal of Honor for saving the lives of twenty-three men as a chaplain in Vietnam.

Now at 70 he was going to jail for a year for joining other protesters in pouring their own blood at the gate of the School of the Americas at Fort Benning, Georgia, which trains military people in violent tactics, usually on behalf of right-wing dictators in Latin America. The crimes of our trainees include the murder of Bishop Oscar Romero as he celebrated Mass in El Salvador, along with the killing of several priests, nuns, and countless simple folk in many, many countries.

There was no press, no TV, only his wife Judy and a few friends who felt that we should be going to prison with him. In a world with a notable shortage of heroes, we were thankful to be supporting one. Any courage we may have claimed for ourselves was dissolved by the act of this quiet priest.

We left grateful to our friend, but most of all grateful to God from whom all blessings flow, especially Charles Liteky, still God's priest. Released from prison in 2001 and then faced by the Iraq war, Charlie was where you'd expect him to be—in the middle of Baghdad doing "grunt" work in a hospital.

THE LAST SERMON

But the day of the Lord will come like a thief. . . .

2 PETER 3:10

It won't be the first time I have overrated something I've done, but I think last Sunday's sermon was one of my better efforts. Among other things, I asked if Jesus would perform a lethal injection for capital punishment, and no one accused me of preaching politics.

Afterwards, I was sorry that I did not tape it or ask someone to turn on the church's tape recorder. Then I wondered, just why do I preach anyway? Am I trying to say something immortal that must be recorded, or am I trying to please God in some small way? How important is the opinion of God to me?

Growing old should at least set off a warning alarm that I might not have too much time to get my motives and priorities straight. Someday, before I am ready, I will preach my last sermon; and I hope that I will not worry much about whether it was taped, but instead, was it okay with God?

When I have carelessly preached and ministered, any other boss would have justifiably fired me. But God's mercy and patience continue as God lets me try to represent the holy. It's pure human arrogance, except that God's grace always comes to the undeserving.

THE COMPOST PILE

God, grant me the serenity to accept
the things I cannot change;
courage to change the things I can;
and wisdom to know the difference.

SERENITY PRAYER OF
ALCOHOLICS ANONYMOUS

We all suffer physically and emotionally, but most of us try to escape our pain, or throw its lessons away like garbage. But the fact is that garbage makes good compost.

Everyone has experienced a variety of hurts, betrayals, cruel words, and thoughtless acts, intended and unintended. Some of us have been the victims of physical, sexual, or verbal violence. Many words and actions are impossible to forgive except by the grace of God. And many of these are events that we do not want to forget, lest we treat others in the same way as we have been treated.

What to do with all the garbage we have piled up? We can let it smell up our lives, or we can find ways of turning it into a compost pile from which food and flowers grow. If we have suffered verbal violence, we can put the words in our emotional compost pile, and seek the grace never to use them on other people. If we were told as children that we were stupid and would never amount to anything, we can say just the opposite to our children and grandchildren. By reminding them that they are smart (all children are smart in different ways) and loving them unconditionally, we cause something productive to grow out of our own childhood pain. We have paid our dues and refuse to let the pain go to waste.

Pain can make us mean and bitter, or it can make us compassionate. It is a powerful source of energy waiting to be used. Pain can help make us want to tip the scales in favor of love and mercy, offsetting the cruelties that we have experienced. We have often paid heavy dues; it would be a shame to waste them.

Most of us do not change unless it is forced upon us. Early pain can be a graceful force working in us to make our last years our best years. We are hardly masochists when we use our pain well, thanking God that it has not been in vain. People who produce life-enriching works are often people who have suffered much, like Van Gogh, who turned his agony into art. The difference between the person who sits at home nursing his or her pain and the person who makes the most of her last days is that the latter uses her pain creatively.

We can grow some beautiful things from our compost pile of life's hurts and troubles.

The Little Orange Model A

In my Father's house are many rooms . . .
I go to prepare a place for you.

John 14:2

When I was a boy, our family frequently drove from Minneapolis to Chicago, where my grandparents lived and where my father's employer was headquartered. Once we got caught in an unseasonable blizzard outside of Madison, Wisconsin. We joined a long line of snowbound vehicles whose drivers decided that a bright orange Model A Ford coupe with a Shell Oil insignia would be the first to break through the snowdrifts.

When it got stuck, the other drivers would jump out and push it through the snow. Then they would pile back in their cars and follow the Model A's tracks. We kids cheered because we knew that when the Model A broke through the snowdrifts, we would too.

People leave soul tracks for us to follow. They do not tell us how to do things or how to think; rather they become an inspiration, a trailblazer for us. As we age and become more vulnerable, life's struggles can open our eyes to people who are God's pioneers. We sense that Jesus and others have been here and gone ahead of us to prepare a place for us.

What's It All About, Joe?

Remembrances of Joe Sittler, wrestler with God,
friend of the earth, friend

We sat in "Jimmy's," a little beer joint on
55th Street a block down from the Lutheran
School of Theology in Chicago, a favorite
hangout for students and faculty. Joe and I
ordered two dark beers and crunched the pea-
nut shells littered on the floor as we walked
to a table in the corner, where we enjoyed a
few laughs and tried to make some sense of
our aging lives.

"What's it all about, Joe? Are you afraid to
die?" His spontaneous reply could be chis-
eled in marble. Later when he repeated it on
tape, it was almost word for word the same.

The fear of death, I'm convinced, is at
the bottom of all apprehensions. To

say of any of us that we do not fear death is a lie. To be human is to fear death. To love life is to hope and to wish not to leave it. And all people fear death. I think that it is one of the most creative fears there is because it bestows a value, an affection and a gratitude for life which otherwise there would not be. That is what the Psalm [90] means by the statement, "So teach us to number our days that we may get a heart of wisdom."

"Take off your theological hat, Joe. What do you feel in your gut about your own death?"

My 80-year-old friend and mentor smiled. "What a waste," he replied.

A lanky 6' 3" with a Mt. Rushmore profile, Joe was first a parish pastor, then, for most of his career, a theological professor. When most people his age barely made the shuffle-board circuit, he still counseled students and gave memorable sermons and lectures from coast to coast. His brain was his library and manuscript. Legally blind and with a hearing aid that emitted an eerie sound, Joe demonstrated the reality of grace. "I can keep going as long as I can read the big, red American Airlines sign," he said. Jeanne—musician, composer, wife, and mother to two daughters and four sons—kidded that he would preach at his own crucifixion if they would send him the plane fare.

Why begin with death in a conversation with the person many believe was the greatest Lutheran theologian in twentieth-century America? Because in Sittler's upside-down view of things, what a person thinks about death is a good clue as to what he or she thinks about life. And Joe thought much about life, too much according to Barbara, one of his daughters, who once screamed at him, "Dad, stop thinking, will you? That's all you do is think!"

In their younger days, the Sittler family grew too large and too numerous for a Chevy sedan, and the kids pestered Joe to buy a family station wagon like some of their friends' families had. But Joe couldn't afford a station wagon on a Lutheran professor's salary, not one that wouldn't fall apart with six wild-cats disguised as human beings tussling in the back seat.

One day Joe came home driving a big, black, old hearse and the kids went nuts. None of their friends could brag about a family vehicle that gave thousands of people their last ride. Maywood, Illinois was never the same after Papa Joe drove the hearse down the street with six riotous kids playing "cops and mobs."

Away from chauffeuring and lecturing, Joe loved to read, especially anything by Conrad, Melville, Burton, Tolstoy, poets like Gerard Manley Hopkins and Emily Dickinson, and various biographies. After his eyes failed and all the ink spots on a page looked the same to him, he turned to books on tape, but still talked about the books he was "reading." The pictures on television got more and more fuzzy, just like the plots. However, he liked "Gunsmoke" because it didn't simply have good guys vs. bad guys, but some "in-between guys," just like life.

Whatever the assigned topic he never failed to talk about grace, and, for the last years, how it related to death and dying. He taught his hearers to look for the grace notes, or unexpected beats, in each of Jesus' parables, as well as in much of the Bible—indeed in much of life. Joe was curious about everything, from the architectural beauty of Eliel Saarinen's Christ Lutheran Church in Minneapolis, to what kind of manure was best for the trees he planted in the seminary yard. He was not a systematic theologian; he was more of a "seat of the pants" theologian, or as Sister Moira Creede wrote: "With feet planted firmly in midair, Joseph Sittler is prepared to take off in any direction."

It was "the care of the Earth" (a phrase that became the title of one of his books) that most engaged him. Long before ecology became politically correct for many, Joe asked what happens to us when we wantonly destroy our mother, the Earth. Joe's final hope was not in humanity, but in God. "But I do go around planting trees on the campus," he said.

Many who heard him considered that Joe was first and foremost a preacher. Listeners had to stay alert because he often ended where other preachers were just warming up. He preached on Matthew 15: 21–28, about the Canaanite woman who begged Jesus to heal her demon-possessed daughter, but Jesus said that it was not fair to take the children's bread and throw it to the dogs. The Canaanite woman came back with: "Yes, Lord, yet even the dogs eat the crumbs that fall from their masters' table."

Jesus answered her: "O woman, great is your faith! Be it done for you as you desire." Joe paused, then seized upon the grace note and banged it home: "What quality do you suppose Jesus saw in this foreigner, this Canaanite woman, to which he gave the name *faith*?" Then with the timing of Jack Benny, Joe said "Amen," and sat down.

Joe would cut through the nonessentials we confuse with Christian faith and get right to the heart of the matter. In his first book, *The Doctrine of the Word*, he made it clear that he was not a biblical literalist. Jesus Christ, as the word made flesh, not the word made book, ruled for Joe. For example, he once playfully suggested that there was something "fishy about the fish fry" that Jesus was reputed to have had on the beach with his disciples after the resurrection.

I think that Joe believed the resurrection was too frightfully mysterious, too far beyond any human explanation, too foundational to the faith, to reduce it down to whether or not Jesus ate a McDonald's fishburger on the beach with his friends. According to Joe's way of thinking, to explain the resurrection is to trivialize it. He seemed to say that if we know the answer, it's probably because we don't understand the question.

"What's it all about, Joe?" We never fully resolved our Jimmy's beer-joint question, except for his rich words about the fear of death. A few months before he died, he seemed to be still struggling with the ultimate question, like all the rest of us mortals. I decided simply to ask him what he thought happens to us after we die. He paused, then spoke with a finality that said that this was all he could or would say on the subject:

"Paul nailed down the whole business: 'If we live, we live to the Lord, and if we die, we die to the Lord; so then whether we live or whether we die, we are the Lord's.' Now, let's eat."

Author's Note

Dr. Joseph A. Sittler was born in Upper Sandusky, Ohio, on September 26, 1904. The son of a Lutheran pastor, Sittler graduated from Wittenberg University and Hamma Divinity School and served as pastor of Messiah Lutheran Church in Cleveland Heights, as professor of theology at the Chicago Lutheran School of Theology in Maywood and at the Chicago Divinity School, and upon retirement, as theologian-in-residence at the Lutheran School of Theology in Chicago. He authored several books, including *Grace Notes and Other Fragments* and *The Care of the Earth.* He was the husband of Jeanne Sittler and the father of two daughters and four sons. Joe died seated in his big leather lounge chair in Chicago on December 28, 1987.